A Christian's Perspective

Journey through Grief

Shelia E. Lipsey
Cover design by Hazel Morgan

A Christian's Perspective

Journey through Grief

Shelia E. Lipsey
Cover design by Hazel Morgan

PUBLISHED BY:
BRENTWOOD CHRISTIAN PRESS
4000 BEALLWOOD AVENUE
COLUMBUS, GEORGIA 31904

DEDICATION

This book is dedicated to my beloved fiancé Roderick V. Elmore (1956-1997). Roderick I will love you for Always, Now and Forever. I look forward to seeing you in that majestic heavenly place that God is preparing for those who love Him. You taught me what a love from God truly is. Even though I did not get the chance to bear your name, in my heart you are my husband, my gift from God. You loved me unconditionally and I will forever be thankful to God for allowing us to share our lives and love with each other.

I also dedicate this book to all those who have experienced the loss of a loved one. May you find and know that our God is an ever-present help in times of trouble. He will never leave us or forsake us.

I most definitely dedicate this book to my Lord and Savior Jesus Christ. Thank you Lord for inspiring me to write this book, for giving me the words to say and the strength to say them. I love you Lord with all of my heart and with all of my soul. I thank you Lord for saving me and that one day I too will be with you in that beautiful heavenly city, my eternal home.

ACKNOWLEDGMENTS

To my mother, Cora Ann Bell

Momma, thank you for everything. Thank you for being by my side through every situation in my life, the good and the bad, the sad times and the glad times. Thank you for teaching and instilling in me that I truly can do ALL things through Jesus Christ who strengthens me. Thank you for believing in me and for supporting me. Of all the mothers God created, He formed you, predestined you, chose you, and elected you to be my mother. And for this, I can never ever begin to thank Him enough! I love you mommie dearest. I love you!

Your baby,

Shelia

FOREWORD

When we lose someone we love it is often the most painful experience a person will face and have to endure. It is most often an experience that attacks us in ways we have never known. Now you're the one who finds yourself having to face it—*THE DEATH OF A LOVED ONE.*

You may not know how you will face living life without your loved one. If you are that someone who is now experiencing life without the one you love, then I have written this book just for you; just for us. I am not writing about something that others have told me about grief, even though I have spoken to many persons who have experienced grief. I am writing from firsthand experience. I am writing from my heart. I have tried to be as candid as I possibly can in describing my own journey through grief in hopes that it will provide some help, some understanding, and some minute comfort to you. I am still in the healing stages myself. I am still traveling on my journey through grief so this book has been quite difficult for me to write.

As Christians, we might feel that we are supposed to be this strong tower of strength that is immovable and invincible because we have the Lord our God on our side and in our lives. This is not always the case. In fact, as believers, we might experience or feel just the opposite because we don't understand why a God who loves us would allow such a painful, heartbreaking sorrow to enter into our lives. But it happens even to us, and it can leave us feeling crushed, brokenhearted and perplexed.

I was lead by the Holy Spirit to write this book to you. I hope that by reading it, you will see that each of us at some time or other more than likely will walk the journey through grief because each of us must answer that call one day. But if we *do* have God on our side, we have the One who will lead us with his love, compassion and unfathomable mercy and grace.

Be encouraged, my friend. God has never left you or your loved one. God is yet here for us. And with his help, you will find that Life Does Go On Even After Losing Someone you Love.

CONTENTS

Let me not grieve
As if I have no future hope
But instead let me lean on the
One, who through it all,
Will help me learn just how to cope.

Shelia E. Lipsey

1

WHEN DEATH BREAKS IN

There is now another moment in time that will forever be etched in my mind. It has caused me to begin yet another journey through grief in addition to the one I have been traveling for the past several years. That event happens to be the September 11, 2001 terrorist attack on the United States of America.

As you know, thousands of lives were lost on that day and countless people have been affected by this devastating act. Many of us laid down our heads the night before looking forward to the next day, or perhaps we lay down with worry and concerns filling our minds; maybe we went to sleep that night full of love and happiness, peace and contentment. A single mom tucked in her little one; a husband snuggled closely against the warmth of his wife; a wife looked upon her sleeping husband; friends chatted on the phone until early dawn; and on and on. I don't know what the case might have been but I can say that I don't think any one of us expected what was to come early on the morning of September 11th. The day that so many lives would be changed forever.

For me, when the reality of what had taken place began to settle in my mind, I was harshly reminded once more how temporary this journey called life truly is. How death doesn't give us any forewarning, hint or sign. It bombards its way into our lives leaving behind a track of hurt, sadness, and brokenness. It doesn't ask our permission to enter; it just boldly, without fear or apprehension invades our lives and destroys our world as we know it. It doesn't care how we feel about our loved ones; how we will ache at the loss of our loved one. It doesn't care. It just comes and breaks in and breaks us.

When I listened and watched the news on the morning of September 11, and thereafter, I experienced the cut of the knife called grief as it began to once more spread across my already broken heart. I felt deep stabbing pains of hurt, sorrow and tears that the families of these loved ones were now gripped by. I cried the tears that the little ones cried as they realized their mommy or daddy would not be coming back home. I felt the sting of death as thousands searched and roamed the streets of New York, hoping and praying that it wasn't their loved one. I tried to tell myself like I did once before that what I saw must be a huge mistake, a cruel joke or that this must be a nightmare that I would be awakened from soon. I felt the same false ray of hope that so many began to feel themselves, as they wanted desperately to believe that they would find their spouses, significant others or children safe and unharmed. I ached and I ached over all that lay ahead for those who were now going to travel the journey that I knew too well.

God! Why I screamed out. What is happening Lord? Why this Father? Again, the same concerns, the same old doubts and fears tried to creep inside my spirit. The same anger and bitterness that consumed me before seemed to quickly begin wrapping itself around my heart squeezing the little life I had left on this journey.

I saw the faces. Broken, lost, devastated faces. Faces void of existence because when they lost their loved one, a part of their lives were taken too. What can I say to those who are now added to the list of the left behind?

What I can tell you is that life really does go on even after losing someone you love. I am a living, breathing, walking, talking example of such. My loved one is too because he now resides at his eternal glorious home.

But you like me, probably are now saying what I said when I first began traveling my journey through grief. I said, *"Tell it to somebody who cares because you don't know like I know what I've lost and how much I've lost. You don't know how much I hurt and how much I ache. And I don't want to hear you or anyone else tell me that life goes on because life for me has come to a cruel, screeching halt. It has stopped me dead in its tracks and kicked me off the journey of life and thrown me into this journey of grief."* But my response to you is that I do understand. I do feel what you feel. But what I have learned is that no matter what we do, or what we say from this point on, the journey has begun and it did not and will not ask for my permission or your permission because we will travel it nonetheless.

This journey, for those of us who have been left behind to grieve, is now beginning. It is one that will forever be traveled and never forgotten. It makes no difference if we personally knew those who were murdered, stolen from us by death itself. It makes do difference if like me, you grieve because you already know the pain of losing a loved one. Or maybe it's because we know that the road ahead will be a tough one to travel.

2

GRIEF EXPRESSED

My beloved fiancé, Roderick, died in 1997 at the age of 41. He was the victim of a brutal beating and murder. I remember as if it happened today, right now.

The days preceding his death were beautiful although when I look back, I can hear in Roderick's voice that he seemed to have had some premonition of his death. I have heard people say such things as this many times after the death of a loved one. But now, I too, can add my name to this list.

Rod knew the pain and anguish I had suffered throughout my life. I felt trapped by what I felt was an unfair hand that was dealt me by life and even by God. I had not only physical problems but fought the bitter past of failed relationships. Rod was always the one to encourage me and tell me to put the past behind me and "Put God First" and before me. "Then and only then," he would say, "can you move from the past and live in today, Shelia."

Two days before his brutal murder, he told me these same words. "Shelia," he said, "I want you to always remember to "Put God First. Always remember that only God can and will see you through." I didn't understand at that time the effect his last words would have on my life. I just believe he sensed that something was about to happen. There were even times in the preceding months when Rod told me that he would never leave me, unless he was killed. I did not want to hear him talking like that and would often tell him so. But his reply would be "Well, it could very well happen, Shelia. Tomorrow is promised to no man and there is so much violence in the world today that you just don't know what another person has on his mind." Yet he never spoke fearfully. He had such deep trust and faith in God and so he believed that death was just the door that would lead him to his "real home." He wasn't fatalistic or anything. He was faithful and trusting and just believed God. Time and time again his words would ring and ring throughout my ears, throughout my mind and within my spirit.

After Roderick's death, I was totally devastated and even today, and now even years later, I find that I still experience the devastating effects of losing him. I am experiencing, like many of you, the ultimate pain—the pain of grief because I lost an essential part of my life when I lost Roderick.

In his book, *"A Grief Observed,"* C. S. Lewis described the pain and grief of losing his wife by saying,

"No one ever told me that grief felt so like fear. I am not afraid, but the sensation is like being afraid. The same fluttering in the stomach, the same restlessness, the yawning, I keep on swallowing. What does it matter now whether my cheek is rough or smooth? They say an unhappy man wants distractions—something to take him out of himself. ... It's easy to see why the lonely become untidy; finally, dirty, and disgusting."

I know for myself what C. S. Lewis felt like when his wife died. I have experienced the same anguish that he experienced and that you are experiencing now. Like Lewis, I too felt that it was not worth fixing myself up, making myself look presentable, or taking the time to clean the house or cook a meal or bathe, or anything that involved "living." Why would I continue to do these things when my beloved was gone?

When Roderick was taken away from me, the weight of pain nearly drove me to suicide. I became a living zombie. I felt my heart had literally been broken and crushed. I became consumed with anger and doubt. I felt God had deserted not only me but my dear Roderick as well. The God I so proudly proclaimed to others as sovereign became a God who I believed had betrayed Roderick and me.

On the day that he was murdered, he had just gotten word that he had been blessed with a great new job that would open the door even wider for him to accomplish the things in life he desired.

We were actively involved in our church. Roderick worked with the Outreach Ministry and I worked in our Children's Church Ministry. He was a much-loved man and filled with a heart of genuine concern and deep care for others.

After not ever having a relationship with their biological father, my sons had come to love him as their own father. My family thought he was the best thing that could ever happen to me and they were right! I loved him with all of my heart. I was so grateful to God for designing our lives to intertwine with each other.

Rod and I had not been dating a very long time when he asked me to marry him. But I knew that this man was from God. I felt it in my spirit and after much prayer one on one with God and after praying alongside Roderick, we knew we were about to make the step God wanted us to take. So when Roderick asked me to become his wife, I accepted and the two of us began making plans for our wedding day. I was excited at the fact that not only was I going to have a wonderful Christian mother-in-law but a Christian husband too, who loved my sons and me dearly and whom we loved also. Our wedding day was planned to take place on my birthday. Yet two months before that day, on May 28, 1997, Roderick was beaten and shot by thugs trying to take what rightfully belonged to him.

I was torn into. I was destroyed. I began to live my own day-to-day death. I became consumed with bitterness, hate, and unforgiveness. I wanted desperately to understand what happened. Why had God allowed such a tragedy as this to happen? How could he have taken Roderick away from family, from friends, from so many people who loved him? How could he take him away from me-the very one who needed him, who lived and breathed him? How could he take him away after bringing us together?

I wanted vengeance for the people who stole his life away and destroyed our dreams and aspirations. I felt numb, like a zombie, emotionless, and empty. So many different emotions all at one time consumed my very being. Where is God? I cried out. And why did he hate me so much? Why did he not let Roderick live instead of dying? Why, why, why my heart and soul cried out.

In the onset of your grief experience you might very well go through these same feelings. Feelings of anger, doubt, loneliness, unforgiveness and pain might consume you. God may seem to be far away while pain rampages through your entire body, mind and soul.

It matters not how your loved one died. It only matters that the person you loved, whether wife, husband, mother or father, sibling or child is no longer here on earth with you and beside you. He or she is unreachable, vanished, never to be with you again. And it hurts like no other hurt you have ever experienced or will ever experience in your life.

You think because you are a Christian that your pain will be any less? You think that your thoughts of anger and doubt will not be as great? I am here to tell you that it is not so. I'm also here to tell you that everything you feel during your journey through grief and pain, God understands. You might even become bitter, like I did, and like me you might even say, "Sure, God understands. But you don't know like I know."

That's where you're wrong. I do know. After all, I have walked in your shoes, treaded the same ground as you. We have lost someone we love. Therefore, we do share a commonality. That commonality is—Grief, loss, hurt and the ultimate pain.

Where were you when I laid the earth's foundations?
Tell me, if you understand, Who marked off its
dimension? Surely you know! Who stretched a
measuring line across it? On what were its footings set,
or who laid its cornerstone while the morning stars
sang together and all the angels shouted for joy?
Who shut up the sea behind doors when it burst forth
from the womb, when I made the clouds its garment and
wrapped it in thick darkness, when I fixed limits for it,
and set its doors and bars in place, when I said,
This far you may come and no farther,
Here is where your proud waves halt?

Job 38: 4-18 NIV

3

IS GOD REAL?

You may find yourself questioning, as I did, the existence of God. I became truly angry, mad, and furious at Him. You may find yourself saying within or even out loud, "Where is my God? Where is he now?" As for me, I didn't know what had struck. I only knew that everything was gone. My life had abruptly come to an endless, screeching halt! Nothingness settled in as the grief of pain overwhelmed me. Because I had never doubted God, I became even angrier.

If God is sovereign, I thought, why did He allow a true Christian man like Roderick to be brutally murdered?

Each day I am reminded and must live with the knowledge, the hurt, the pain, and the grief of remembering that he is no longer with me. Each day, the screams of my broken heart yell from every fiber of my soul.

C. S. Lewis explained it so much better when he said, "I not only live each endless day in grief, but live each day thinking about living each day in grief."

The fear of living each day without your loved one, at times can become unbearable. It might be hard, difficult to talk to your family, friends or children because they don't know how to deal with your hurt and after all, they too are traveling the journey as well. Sure, in the very beginning, the early stages of your grief, family and friends try to be sympathetic. But that quickly changes as people go on with their lives and you are left still reeling from the loss of your loved one.

The sympathetic words and phone calls and visits begin to fade as the days turn into weeks. You may begin to feel as if no one really cared in the first place. No one really understands just how hurt and devastated you are. No one cares. You are left in despair and sometimes the anger can start to consume you. The emptiness can start to eat away at you. The tears begin to leave deep streaks in your skin and you feel there is no life left in you.

As for me, I began to feel that I was a walking advertisement for a cruel new game God had invented called "let's see how much pain Shelia can bear." I asked God, "Is this some kind of test? Well, if it is, I'm no Job and I don't want to be like Job," I thought. Again and again, I asked Him why He allowed such happiness to enter my life, such true unconditional love, only to snatch it away from me. After all, Roderick was my foundation, my supporter, my strong tower, my gift from God and my best friend.

All I can tell you my friends is that, we, as Christians, must cling to the knowledge, to the fact, that we are children of the King; the King of all Kings. Surprisingly, the more I poured out my feelings, my anger, and my emotions to God, I soon began to see Him in a different aspect. I began to realize that he does share in my pain. He does understand my hurt and sorrow. He does understand about each tear that falls from my weary eyes. God does understand my friend.

When my thoughts turned to Roderick, which was continually, I began to remember how God was with him, imbedded in him. I remembered the love Roderick had for God. I remembered how he cried out his heart to God each and everyday. I remembered how he was always striving to walk closer to God. I remembered his longings and pleadings to God to help him to become a better person, to become more Christian in his heart. When I dwelt on these thoughts I slowly began to see once more that everything God does *is* good. But this did not happen overnight, my friends. It is a journey. A journey through grief.

To weep
is to make less
The depth of grief.

William Shakespeare

4

ALLOW YOURSELF TO GRIEVE

Allow yourself to grieve. Allow yourself to cry. Allow yourself to hurt. Allow yourself to doubt. Allow yourself to feel anger and even betrayal. Only in allowing yourself to feel your pain can your life go on. But only in time.

The relationship and friendship between Roderick and me was perfect. I didn't say that Roderick was perfect or that I was perfect. I said our relationship was perfect. It was based on our unconditional love for each other given to us by God. I envisioned us spending years together, growing old together, but it was not to be. Our relationship lasted all of six months before Roderick went home to be with God. I could not understand how such a man as he could be taken away in what I believed was before his time. After all, Roderick was in the prime of his life. As I told you, the day he was murdered, he had just been notified that he had gotten the job he had applied for a few weeks earlier. That job was to be our ticket to living a more prosperous life. We were going to pay off bills, do some of the things we wanted and planned to do. We were going to become Mr. And Mrs. Elmore. What more could a girl ask for than to find the man of her dreams. The one who loves her just because? The one that was given to her as a precious gift from an all-loving God?

How dare God do this, I cried. Why, Roderick was only 41 years old! He had not yet fulfilled the desires of his heart, achieved the dreams and goals that we had planned for our lives together. He had not experienced the joy of growing old, of seeing the hands of time move slowly over our lives and our love.

We never had the chance to say, "I do." This cut me like a knife over and over again.

Did he die before his time? I truly believe he did. I did not say that God did not have control over Roderick's death or that it was a mistake of some kind that Roderick died when he did. I just believe that one can die before his/her time but never before God's time. I honestly believe that before God allows his child, his heir, the one he has adopted into his fold, his sheep, to stray to far off the track, or mess up a little much or steer too long in the wrong direction, that God will take that person on home to be with him in glory. I don't have any proof of this; I just know that I believe once saved always saved. I just know that God's mercies are new every morning and He is full of grace and does not want to see His children continue to stumble and wallow in this sin-sick world. You see because we belong to God we are in the world, but not of the world.

You too, might believe that God allowed your loved one to leave this earth before he or she had a chance to marvel at God's creation, before he or she had time to enjoy life and living, love and happiness, sunshine and rain. Again, it is alright to have these thoughts, to feel that God has been unfair. Our God is a big God. He can take our questions, our thoughts and our pain any way we dish it out.

Don't let anyone tell you that you should not question God. As Christians, God is our father and we are His children. Haven't you at one time or another questioned your parents, your friends your family, your employer, your teacher about something you didn't quite understand or perhaps agree with? Well, if we truly do have a personal relationship with God, our father, we can ask him what we will. He wants us to come to him with our doubts, with our questions. He is our Father and He already knows what we are thinking. He already knows how we feel anyway. So why not question him? Why not pour it all out to Him?

I have also come to the realization that God *allows* my pain too, and that God is indeed God—He is in control. I began to see, perhaps weeks, perhaps months after Rod's death that praise was in order, and that God was and is the giver of life but Satan is the author of death.

I cannot pinpoint when this realization resurfaced in my life because grief caused me to lose all perspective of time. I do know that I often times described Roderick as my "gift from God." Did the death of my love, my best friend, my husband, open my spirit to see what is so obvious? That God is a great giver of love? Somehow, I believe it did. It was in not having Roderick with me that made me see that he truly was a precious gift.

5

LONGING FOR GOD'S RETURN

As I live each day without Roderick, my life has now taken on a drastic change. I long for God's return and have become more keenly aware of how temporary this life on earth truly is. This earth is not our home. It is merely a guesthouse in which we temporarily reside as our heavenly Father makes preparations for our homecoming. Yet, within myself, I began to question just why I longed for God's return.

I have secretly asked myself if I long for God's return because I know it will be the only way I will see my dear, sweet Roderick again. I am afraid of the answer of which I know lurks in my heavy, grieved heart. Yet I know that I will be with the Father who we both love. I will see God's radiance shine upon me and feel myself bathed in His awesome love for all of eternity.

As I live each day without Roderick, my thoughts about God and His omnipotence have continued to increase. I find my thoughts are focusing more on God and His sovereignty. I now feel a source of strength in thinking of God and the fact that Roderick is with Him.

As C. S. Lewis realized that he was focusing more on God, a remarkable thing happened. He began to see his wife everywhere. Not in a literal sense did he see her everywhere, but he could feel her presence in him and round about him wherever he went. Just like Lewis, I too see Roderick. I see him in the words of my sons, in the gait of a stranger, in the encouraging voice of a co-worker, in the smile of a friend.

Do you too now find yourself longing for God's return? For Him to come and take you away from the troubles and heartaches of this world? Do you long for Him to come remove you far and away from this place and on to your eternal home? If you do, have you questioned, like me, why you anticipate that day or feel like you want to hurry it along? I believe it is because the pain we are experiencing on our journey through grief seems so unbearable and so unfair. Perhaps, we might feel that we don't know how much more sorrow we can stand. The scripture, "God doesn't put any more on us than we can bear" seems to be far from the truth.

But if we stop for a moment, we will see that God is indeed walking with us through our journey of grief. We have made it thus far. We have made it to this day. You have made it to this day, because you are now reading this book. I did not say it is easy. I am only saying that as I go through my journey of grief, I see that I have now made it up to this moment on this journey and I am still going on.

You too will make it through. God is seeing to that at every moment, of every minute of every day. Yield your broken vessels to Him. Yield all of you to Him. He is big enough to handle it all.

I do believe that we as believers should anticipate Christ's return. I believe that we should not look to earth as our final home. Earth is the "stop pit." It is here that God has purposed for us to reside for a short time. We who remain here have a work to do for God! But we still should really look deep within ourselves and be true to our own selves about why we are in eager anticipation for his coming.

I think this can be a good thing in its own way because we do have assurance that we will be with Him. Unlike those who don't know Christ, we do know Him. Therefore, we can rest assured that He will provide our every need until He comes back for us. Until that day, be strong and of good courage.

The Lord is my Shepherd; I shall not be in want,
He makes me lie down in green pastures,
He leads me beside quiet waters,
He restores my soul.
He guides me in paths of righteousness
For his name's sake.
Even though I walk
Through the valley of the shadow of death,
I will fear no evil, for you are with me;
Your rod and your staff they comfort me.
You prepare a table before me
In the presence of my enemies,
You anoint my head with oil;
My cup overflows;
Surely goodness and love
Will follow me all the days of my life,
And I will dwell
In the house of the Lord forever.

Psalm 23 NIV

6

DO YOU FEAR DEATH?

I don't believe Roderick was actually afraid to die. However, at the moment of death, I can't say if he truly was or not. As for me, I can honestly say that I am not afraid of death, but I cannot say that I am not afraid of dying. I know that when death comes for me that I will be escorted to my heavenly home, my eternal home instantaneously. But my flesh still has a fear of dying itself.

My consolation in Roderick's death is to know that he immediately went to be with God. Scripture tells us that "To be absent from the body is to be present with the Lord." Hang on to this my friends. Hang on to it with all you have inside of you. Know that those who die in the Lord go to be with God, the Father immediately, in an instant, in the twinkling of an eye. This in and of itself provides deep consolation for me and it can for you as well. It doesn't make any difference if that person made a multitude of mistakes and committed a multitude of sins during his/her lifetime. It doesn't matter whether it was a newborn baby or an elderly person. It doesn't' matter what the world thinks of that person. All that matters is the relationship that person had with God our savior. God does not keep a record of our wrongs just so he can throw it up in our face. When he sent his son to die on a cross on a hill called Calvary, Jesus, the son, died for the sins of the past, present and future. He died so that we might live. I'm so glad that Roderick knew this and believed this!

I even think about what Roderick is doing in heaven. I would like to believe, like to think, that he is rejoicing in the Lord, that he is having a great and marvelous time among the Savior he loves so much. I also would like to think that he is by God's side helping him prepare a place for me and all of us who die in the Lord.

26

The word of God tells us that in heaven there is no more crying, no more death, no more pain and no more sadness. Knowing that Roderick has finally escaped the evil trappings of this earthly world, with all of its envy, jealously, violence and corruption, gives me somewhat a sense of inner peace.

You might have your own feelings about what your loved one is doing as he or she celebrates eternal life with God. There are so many things that run through our minds when we are faced with the death of a loved one. We can, however, rest assured that they will return with God when he comes for us, His saints. God tells us that he will bring our loved ones in Christ along with him to meet us in the sky. I rejoice in this fact. I rejoice in the very fact that Roderick will be in the heavens to greet me. And not only Roderick, but my father and grandmother as well.

You too can rest assured of this fact. This is not something that we have to think will happen or hope will happen. It is something that we know will happen. It is one of the many promises of God. After he comes for us, then we shall receive our glorified bodies. Bodies that will no longer decay or die. Bodies that will no longer experience broken-heartedness, grief, pain, sorrow and loneliness. We will live victorious lives in the eternal realm with our loved ones and most importantly with God!

During your grief experience, it might be hard to think on these things because you are so tormented with the pain of grief. But as time goes on my friend, your mind will begin to think on more heavenly things, on the promises of God if you allow it to. You may even develop a far greater and deeper insight into the spiritual realm as I have.

In talking with others who are experiencing grief, I have learned that their pain has been much like mine.

A woman who lost her 34-year-old son to a sudden illness said she felt totally helpless. The pain was overwhelming. She described it as, "a throbbing pain that went to the core of my very being."

When Tamara's brother committed suicide at the age of 24, she said that she felt anger because he never told her goodbye. She couldn't understand what would drive him to commit such an act as suicide. He left behind not only his parents and sisters, but also a two-year old son. "What pain was he enduring that would make him take his own life?" She asked painfully. There were so many things he didn't get to do. She felt his adult life was just beginning and it should have been easy for him to move forward than to not try.

When Cheryl's father died of lung cancer, she said everything was overwhelming. "Even though our family knew he was dying, it still did not prepare me for that day when he took his last breath." Like many others, she felt that she did not get the chance to tell him how she felt about him and how proud she was of him. "It was only God's mercy and strength that got me through that first week," she said.

Patricia's son murdered his own sister when she was 21 years old. She had two small children. Not only is this woman continuing to grieve over the tragic death of her daughter, but she is also grieving over her son who sits in jail because of this heinous crime. Even though he is still alive, can you even begin to imagine the burden, sorrow and heartache she is experiencing? How her love and her heart must be torn. Even I cannot fathom the depth of her despair and hurt. She said, "Not a day goes by that I don't think of my daughter. My daughter, though she was only 21 years old, was my backbone. I cry almost every day over her death. Then I cry some more over the fact that it was my son who took her life. All I can do is ask God to help me and there are days I just don't think I can take much more." But Patricia is still here, still coping, even in the midst of her grief. She is drawing closer to God because of this tragedy that entered her life. There are still times she says, that guilt eats away at her like a cancer.

Guilt over what we could have done or should have done or might have done or should have said, or shouldn't have said can play in our minds like a broken record.

As for me, I play the scene of Roderick's death over and over in my mind as well. I too, longed to tell him good-bye, to hear his last words, to hold him close and tell him how much he was loved. I often think that maybe my love was not strong enough, not deep enough. Maybe he thought that he wasn't loved and ran freely to death's arms. Maybe this life was too much for him to

28

bear. Maybe he didn't fight hard enough against the waiting arms of death. I can't tell you how many painful thoughts ran through my mind and still I experience these kinds of thoughts even now.

My friend, all the pain I have experienced throughout my life could not prepare me for such a thing as losing him. "If onlys" consumed my mind. If only I could change that dreadful night's events. If only he had stayed home a little longer on that fateful evening. If only, if only, if only. But if only does not change the course of events, my friends. The heartbreaking fact is that Roderick is gone from this earthly place, gone forever from the physical. He has left behind his loved ones who still continue to deal painfully with his untimely, tragic departure.

So death can produce fear in us because we are human. Our flesh does not understand or comprehend. Our finite minds lead us to think fearful thoughts. Since Satan is the author of death, I believe it is natural that we will think of death and be afraid. But I tell you now, that you don't have to be afraid of dying.

You don't have to think that your loved one was afraid when death came to claim him/her. I believe that the angels of God come for God's own. I believe that when we close our physical eyes in death, that we are greeted with the most beautiful, the most angelic hosts of heavenly beings that we can't possibly begin to understand or know just how magnificent they really and truly are. I'm sure their majesty and beauty is miraculous, inconceivable!

I believe that Roderick was so at peace and so in awe of all the majesty and beauty of God's creation that there was no fear. After all, fear is of the devil. It is what Satan wants us to believe. He wants us to focus on all that will trap us and instill doubt in our hearts and minds. But God is a loving God. All God does is good and it is all based on His love for our loved ones and us.

It is my earnest prayer that you begin, as I do now, to believe that at the moment, that the very moment our loved ones closed their eyes in death, that there was no fear and trembling but instead they were surrounded by God's mercy, love, grace and beauty, to be ushered into a land that is so beautiful that it is beyond our very finite thought pattern!

I am worn out from groaning;
All night long
I flood my bed with weeping
and drench my couch with tears

Psalm 6:6

7

FEELING BAD ABOUT
FEELING BETTER

In the midst of somewhat better days and happy memories comes the tidal wave of grief's pain. It often sneaks upon you suddenly and without warning. It hits you like a thunderbolt, strong and forceful, knocking you to your very knees.

As the months went by after Roderick's death, I began to feel somewhat better and at the same time felt that I was wrong for feeling better. Even though I didn't want to feel the pain of grief for the rest of my life, I still believed that each time I began to feel better, that in some way I was being unfaithful—unfaithful to Roderick, to our love, and to all that we shared and were planning to share in this earthly life. I didn't want to betray him. I didn't want to forget his love. I didn't want to forget his tender kiss and his affectionate embrace. I didn't want to forget his smile and his compassion. I didn't want to forget.

I didn't even want to forget the way he died. I wanted to remember those who took his life. I wanted to see them suffer and hurt and be filled with torment. I wanted each of their days and all of their nights to be days and nights of torture and pain over what they had done. I didn't ever want to feel better toward them.

Perhaps each of you during your journey through grief will have these same thoughts and emotions. Grief is the ultimate pain and we want it to leave us alone. But we also don't want to forget all that we shared with our loved one(s). This would be for us the ultimate betrayal.

The memories of Roderick's life and our relationship will forever be a part of me. I think about him each and every day. What is different is now I can think about him without crying all the time. There are times I can even talk about him and not cry. But there are also days and moments when the tears and pain appear once more. I believe that I will forever grieve for Roderick, but my grieving will not be as painful. It's almost as if I have begun to accept grief's presence in my life and have adapted to it.

All I can say to you my friends is that, I know that God is love and that He truly possesses all knowledge, all power and all understanding. I know that He is in control of every situation, no matter how devastating. Even though the pain of grief is tremendous and ever present, I know that God is omnipotent, omnipresent and omniscient. I also know that I must stop longing to have Roderick back with me because that is selfish on my part. I know that he is indeed at peace in his eternal home.

When I find myself feeling somewhat better, coping better, reaching out for support and encouragement again, then I must not allow the enemy to place guilt upon my shoulders. The journey of grieving is enough. Do not allow Satan to add the burden of guilt to what is already a painful experience.

When we find ourselves once again smiling at some remark someone made, or waking up and our loved one is not the first thing on our minds as he/she has been, then rejoice in God. He is holding us up, carrying our pain and our sorrows. He is providing us with the strength we need at that moment and for that moment. He is delivering us from the pain little by little, day by day. He is with us as we travel our journey through grief. He is healing us, repairing us. For this we must be thankful instead of feeling bad about feeling better.

Satan wants us to stay down. He wants us defeated. He wants us to stay broken and crushed. But God wants us whole again. God wants joy for us again and peace for us again. He wants us to totally lean and depend on Him. He wants us to be able to help someone else through his or her grief experience, and to be able to say to him/her, "Life Does Go On After Losing Someone You Love."

I will not die, but live
and will proclaim
what the Lord has done.

Psalm 118: 18

8

WE STILL HAVE WORK TO DO

Each moment we live as believers we have the opportunity to win others to Christ. We have the opportunity, the chance to become more like Him, to become stronger in our faith, in our belief. Each moment He allows us to live and breathe on this earth is a moment to fulfill our earthly mission—to tell others about His undying, everlasting love for us.

I have pondered over the circumstances surrounding Roderick's death. I think often of all those who were involved in destroying his life. I did not want to forgive them. I wanted to see them pay. I wanted to see them destroyed. I did not want them to be saved. I did not want them to go to heaven. I did not want any good thing for them. It is only because of the grace and mercy of God that I have begun to let go of the hurt, the anger and the bitterness that settled in my life towards these individuals who stole Roderick's life from not only me, but from his family and friends.

I am continuing to pray about this because it is only through God that I can truly forgive these people. God wants me to pray for them. God wants me to lift them up so they too will spend eternity with Him. I must tell you that this has been hard for me. It has been a bitter pill for me to swallow. But if I am to be healed from the pain and brokenness, I must let go of the anger and hate.

I had to share this with you to let you know that I have a long way to go on my journey. I do want to be able to forgive them, and to allow God to have His vengeance in His own way and in His own time. I do want to be able to truly pray for their salvation. I ask you to pray for me in this area as well. I know that I am holding back total healing in my life as long as I hold on to the anger and bitterness I have toward those who wronged me, who wronged Roderick. Again, it takes time. I believe God is delivering me day by day from these feelings. If He were not, I don't think I would have been able to share these feelings with you.

My friends, bitterness and anger robs us of living. It robs us of being who we should be in Jesus. It robs us of our blessings. It robs us of the memories of our loved ones because we are consumed by the thoughts of those who have taken them from us or by whatever the circumstances that surrounded their deaths. Even if they died as a result of an illness, we tend to still feel anger and bitterness and that is usually directed toward the doctors, the nurses, our family, and even God. But no matter how your loved one died, you must ask God to deliver you from anything that is not of God.

You see, I want to get better and feel better, not bitter. I want to love instead of hate. I want to be joyful instead of consumed by the fire of anger. I want to truly live and love the way God intended for me, His child, His joint heir and His creation to live and love. Even the word of God states in Psalm 66:18, "if I regard iniquity in my heart, then the Lord will not hear me." I don't know about you but I don't want to be cut off from the ears of God. I want him to hear my cries, to hear my pleas. I want Him to answer me and so I must forgive just as He has forgiven me and like He continues to forgive me.

Don't allow the enemy to keep his foot pressed down upon your heart, squeezing the very life out of you. Don't allow the enemy to overtake you. You still have work to do. You are a soldier, a child of the king! Our loved ones who have died in the Lord are at total peace. God will exact his vengeance upon our enemies and the enemies of our loved ones. "Dearly beloved, avenge not yourselves, but rather give place unto wrath: for it is written, Vengeance is mine;; I will repay, " saith the Lord. Romans 12:19 KJV.

God knows what He is doing. We may not ever understand why He allows things to happen in our lives, but we must trust in Him because everything He allows works out ultimately for our good and always for His glory. I may not ever begin to understand why Roderick died like he did. I may not ever understand God's plans in all of this. But I do know that I believe in God. He is my Father. He is my one true source of help. He is the God of Roderick and all of my loved ones who have gone on before me to be with the Lord. And I am just thankful that God is God and besides Him there is none other. I can't explain it. I just accept God for who he is.

If you are experiencing any of these same feelings, remember to pray to God and ask Him to help you. Ask Him to deliver you from the spirit of unforgiveness, anger and revenge. Ask Him to fill you up with His cup of love until it overflows with forgiveness. Perhaps it's yourself you can't forgive. You might blame yourself for your loved one's death. You might feel that it should have been you instead of your loved one. You might feel hatred and anger and bitterness. You might be furious at God. But I'm here to tell you that you must forgive. You must trust in God. You must. You must. You must. Whatever it is that is keeping you burdened down, strapped down, and choking you off from the deliverance of God, LET IT GO! Don't hold on to it forever and allow it to fester in your life and ultimately rob you of once again having joy and peace in your life.

I have come to understand that I remain here on earth because God is not through with me yet. I still have work to do. You still have work to do. That's why you remain here as well. There are souls that need to be witnessed to. There are people dying everyday unsaved! There are those left here who need to hear our stories and feel our pain so that they too can be delivered. There are those who are thirsty for something and that something is the living water of Jesus Christ and often times they don't even realize it! There are those who need to see Jesus living inside of me and inside of you. They need to see how God is strengthening me even in the midst of my sorrow and my pain.

There is still growing that we have to do. We must grow in our trust in God. We must grow in our thoughts towards God. We must grow in our service towards God. We still have work to do! As children of God, we are left on this earth to share the wonder saving power and majesty of Christ the savior. We are left here to proclaim of His goodness, His mercy, and His forgiveness. We are here to share the gospel of Jesus Christ with a sin sick world. We live in a world that can take the lives of our loved ones without blinking an eye and certainly without remorse. We are living in a world that can kill and destroy lives and families without a thought. We are living in a world that can send planes flying into buildings and destroy thousands upon thousands of innocent lives! WE STILL HAVE WORK TO DO MY FRIENDS!

Perhaps we remain here to help ease the pain of someone else, to share a word of comfort, to say a prayer, to hold a hand, or to soothe a hurt. Most of us still have families that need our love, our care and our attention. We must be here to love them and to help them along life's way. Each of us has a purpose for our lives and we must be about fulfilling that purpose that has been set aside and divinely arranged by God. My friends, we must be about doing the will of God, our Father. That's why we remain here.

Pray about the path that God wants you to travel. Exercise the spiritual gifts he has blessed you with. If you don't know what that spiritual gift is, then ask God to reveal it to you. My friends, our day to see the one true God will come as surely as our loved ones. But until that time, we still have work here on earth to do.

If we live, we live to the Lord;
and if we die, we die to the Lord.
So, whether we live or die,
we belong to the Lord.

Romans 14:8 NIV

9

IF YOU COULD SEE
WHERE I HAVE GONE

I can't remember who sent me this poem, and I guess that's not really important. What IS important is that each time I read it, I find a sense of peace and calmness enter my mind and my spirit. I begin to feel the sweet, sweet presence of my beloved Roderick reminding me of how grand his life is now. I begin to understand somewhat God's plan for his children. I had to share it with you.

"If you could see where I have gone, the beauty of this place, and how it feels to know you're Home, to see the Savior's face. To wait in peace and know no fear, just joy beyond compare, while still on earth you miss me, yet wouldn't want me there.

If you could see where I have gone, had made the trip with me, you would know I didn't go alone, the Savior came with me. When I awoke, He was by my side and said as He touched my hand; hurry! You're going home to a Grand and Glorious land.

If you could see where I have gone, and see what I've been shown, you'd never know another fear or ever feel alone. You'd marvel at the care of God, His hand on every life. And realize He really cares and bears with us each strife. And that he weeps when one is lost, His heart is filled with pain, but Oh, the Joy when one comes home a child at home again!

If you could see where I have gone, could stay a while with me. To share the things that God hath made to grace Eternity. You couldn't ever leave for once heaven's joy you'd know you couldn't bear to walk earth's paths, once Heaven was your home.

If you could see where I have gone, you'd know we'll meet someday and though I'm parted from you now that I'm just away.

And know that I'm home with Him and secure in every way. I'm waiting here at Heaven's door to greet you some sweet day.
(Author Unknown)

10

TO LIVE OR TO DIE –
WHICH IS BETTER?

I was looking through Roderick's bible shortly after his death. One of the verses he had highlighted and underlined was, "But to die is even better—"For me to live is Christ and to die is gain." Living for me, and for you, is a chance to help somebody to have the same chance at eternal life as Roderick, as me and as you and your loved one. But I can't help but say that to go and live with God, to see Roderick and my loved ones once more is a time that I anticipate. For me, to die is gain. To die is the ultimate victory because we who are saved will be dying in the Lord. Does this mean that I have some morbid, fatalistic outlook? No, of course not. It means that I know that when the day, the hour, the time comes for me, then, like my Roderick, I will go to my beautiful and glorious eternal home! It means that all of the evil we have to contend with on this earthly level will be done away with. When I view Roderick's death in this manner, then my heart overflows with joy because he is truly living the life with the Savior who loves Him more than I could ever conceive in my finite mind. And of course you know that we always want the very best for those we love.

Your loved one enjoys these same eternal pleasures that we too should look forward to receiving. Now does this sound morbid? I don't think so.

If we believe that Jesus died and rose again, then surely we can believe that our loved ones will rise again as well. The word even tells us in 1 Thessalonians that Jesus will bring with him those who have "fallen asleep" in Christ.

I do miss Roderick. I long for him. However, my dear brothers and sisters in Christ, let us not allow grief to deprive us of our hope, of our faith and our trust in Christ Jesus. Let us not allow grief to deprive us of all the fond, precious memories we have of our loved ones. Memories that can never be taken away from us except by grief. Grief cleverly tries to restrain us by keeping us saddened, burdened and in pain over losing our loved ones.

I am not telling you that we won't long for our loved ones and miss our loved ones. It does not mean that I won't or don't cry for Roderick or desire his gentle embrace. But it tells you and I that we will see them again. When God returns, He will come down from heaven, with the trumpet call of God and we who are still here, that is, those of us who have not yet died a physical death like our loved ones, will be caught up together with our loved ones and God in the sky. This very passage gives me hope. It gives me a sense of anticipation, even a sense of joy and peace! Herein lies my anticipation.

You too, can experience this same joy and peace in knowing and believing that God does keep His word. Not only will we be with the Lord on his return, but we will also be with our loved ones to reign forever more in our eternal homes.

I don't know; no man knows, when that day will arrive, but be encouraged. That day is indeed coming and I don't believe it will be very long.

Be strong and courageous,
Do not be terrified;
Do not be discouraged,
For the Lord your God
will be with you
wherever you go.

Joshua 1:9 NIV

11

CLING TO GOD

On your journey through grief try, though it may be hard, to cling to the fact that God is close to us, to the brokenhearted. Our spirits and hearts are crushed because of our loss. I am still brokenhearted and crushed in spirit. I would be lying if I said anything different. But again, God tells you, and me if we will listen, that He saves those of us whose spirits are crushed. His eyes are on us, His righteous ones, His children.

I know you will experience times when you don't believe that He truly understands your hurt and your pain. As a believer, having gone through what you are experiencing now, I can reassure you that He is ever present.

When I was forced to face the fact that Roderick was dead, gone, I went into shock. Numbness consumed me. I could feel nothingness surround me. This was a moment in time when God was shielding me. He knew that I would not be able to make it through to now, to share with you my words, my emotions, my pain, and my healing had he not made my mind and body shutdown in shock during the initial time of Roderick's death. Because his death was so brutal and tragic, initially my mind would not have been able to conceive the manner in which he died. I had no time to say good-bye, to hear his last words, to hold him and comfort him. I was robbed of all of that. I believe that I would have committed suicide or lost my sanity. I was actually contemplating suicide during the darkest hours of my grief journey. Thanks be to God, He saw me through and is still bringing me through.

God is doing the same for you too at this very moment. God covers all bases, all points. He will not allow us to be overtaken by the evil tactics of Satan—even though we might feel just the opposite.

We are hard pressed on every side,
but not crushed;
perplexed, but not in despair;
persecuted, but not abandoned;
struck down, but not destroyed.
We always carry around in our body
the death of Jesus,
so that the life of Jesus
may also be revealed in our body.
For we who are alive
are always being given over to death
for Jesus' sake, so that his life
may be revealed in our mortal body.
So then, death is at work in us,
but life is at work in you.

2 Corinthians 4: 8-12

The task is hard
But Lord I will trust you
The way is long
But you will show me what to do
I dare not trust the sweetest frame
But I will lean on Your precious name

Shelia E. Lipsey

12

FAITH VS. TRUST

On our journey through grief, it is also important that we, hard as it might be, hold on to our faith. Faith tells us that we do believe in the power of God. Faith tells us that God is indeed who He proclaims He is. Faith tells us that there is life after death. Faith tells us that if we believe on the Lord Jesus Christ that we are saved. Faith says that God can deliver us from the clutches of grief's attacks. He can restore our brokenness. He can give us peace within our spirits. He can give us joy within our hearts. He can fix us up and carry us through this tremendous pain and hurt that we are experiencing. He can give us the spirit of forgiveness over those who have wronged us. Yes, my friends; faith is a great thing to have.

But what about Trust? Can you trust him? Do you trust him during this journey through grief?

What do I mean by trust you might ask? Well, my friends, trust tells us that not only do we believe in the power of God, but we trust that God will exert his power. We trust that God will deliver us from our pain. We trust God will restore our broken hearts. We trust Him to deliver us from the clutches of grief that holds us down and keeps us bound. We trust that He will give us a spirit of forgiveness. We trust that He will deliver us from anger. We trust that he will deliver us from self-imposed guilt and if onlys. We trust that he will fix us up and bring us through even these darkest of days. We trust that He will give us peace and renewed joy.

Do you see the difference? Faith says, I believe God *can*. Trust says, I know God *will*. And He will, if we allow him to.

During our journey through grief, we may try to hold on to our bitterness, our anger, our resentments, and our unforgiveness.

Even though God understands us, and knows the pain we suffer, we still must not allow ourselves to wallow in deep despair too long. If we do, we leave ourselves open to the attacks of the enemy. The enemy, Lucifer, Satan, the Prince of Darkness, what ever you choose to call him, can come in full force, ready to destroy us completely. The enemy rejoices in our sorrow, but God shares in our sorrows. The enemy laughs at our tears, but God stands ready to wipe the tears from our eyes. The enemy seeks to destroy; but God seeks to restore. The enemy wants us to remain bitter. God wants us to get better. I have not come to this realization overnight. During my journey through grief, I was, as I said earlier, bitter, angry and resentful. But as I continued to cry out to God, he heard me and he is yet delivering me from the bitterness and unforgiveness that has tried to continually take up permanent residence in my heart.

He will deliver you too. He will do as He says. His word tells us that He will never leave us or forsake us. In the book of Luke, he asks "Why are you troubled, and why do doubts arise in your hearts: See My hands and My feet, that is I myself; touch Me and see…." (Luke 24:39a). In this passage of scripture God is reaching out to his disciples. He is doing the same for us today. He wants us to reach out to Him during this difficult journey. His word tells us in Psalm 55:22 that, "He will never allow His righteous ones to be shaken."

Even though this tragedy, this death, has entered our lives, God is yet working everything out for us. Everything that He allows, no matter what, no matter how dark and dismal it is, He will see us through. When we trust in Him, we can stand even through this journey through grief.

When loneliness and fear arise, we can stand when otherwise without Him we would fall and crumble. Without Him we would be crushed by the pain and heartache. Without Him we would have no hope. Without Him we would not be able to bear the sorrows of this life, the sorrows of this death. Without Him, we are indeed hopeless and helpless. But with Him, we are more than conquerors! So get up, dust off, stand tall and put your trust in God!

Then I saw a new heaven and a new earth,
for the first heaven and the first earth
had passed away,
and there was no longer any sea.
I saw the Holy City, the New Jerusalem,
coming down out of heaven from God,
prepared as a bride beautifully dressed
for her husband.
And I heard a loud voice from the throne saying,
"Now the dwelling of God is with men,
and he will live with them.
They will be his people,
and God himself will be with them
and be their god.
He will wipe every tear from their eyes.
There will be no more death or mourning
or crying or pain,
for the old order of things
has passed away.

Revelation 21 1:4 NIV

13

THAT HEAVENLY PLACE

I believe most of us tend to think of Heaven as a far away, remote place where God sits mightily on His throne, overseeing all. It is true; He does reside in Heaven. But not only does He reside in Heaven, but our loved ones are with Him also. Death only ends the earthly life. It does not end all. So when Roderick took his last breath, when your loved one said goodbye to this world and to you, he/she immediately went to reside in his/her new eternal home. I asked you earlier what you thought your loved one might be doing now that he/she is no longer with you in the physical. Let me share a little deeper insight into what I actually visualize.

First, I imagine the beauty of the heavenly city. The city where Roderick, and your loved one(s) now resides. Look at what Revelations 21 beginning at verse 18 states: "The wall was made of jasper, and the city was made of pure gold, as pure as glass. The foundation stones of the city walls were decorated with every kind of jewel. The first foundation was jasper, the second sapphire, the third was chalcedony, the fourth was emerald, the fifth was onyx, the sixth was carnelian, the seventh was chrysolite, the eighth was beryl, the ninth was topaz, the tenth was chrysoprase, the eleventh was jacinth, and the twelfth was amethyst. The twelve gates were twelve pearls, each gate having been made from a single pearl. And the street of the city was made of pure gold as clear as glass." (Rev 21 18-22 NCV) "I did not see a temple in the city, because the Lord God Almighty and the Lamb are the city's temple. The city does not need the sun or the moon to shine on it, because the glory of God is its light and the Lamb is the city's lamp."

There are rivers of the water of life flowing out from the throne of God through the city. The trees of life are along the rivers providing spiritual refreshment. I believe our loved ones in heaven drink from the pure, crystal water of life and taste of the fruit that the trees of life brings forth. There is nothing that isn't perfect in heaven. There is beauty untold, mansions beyond our wildest comprehension and imagination! Everything has been washed and cleaned by the shed blood of the precious lamb of God. God is lifted up and magnified by all his children. He continues to prepare a place for us who will be ushered in to him one day too.

Death may brutally sting us here on earth while we are in our natural bodies. But it is the only way that we can enter into the glorious eternity, the city of the most high God our savior. So while we grieve here, our loved ones are rejoicing in that heavenly place with God our savior. While we cry tears of hurt and pain here over the death of our loved one(s), our loved ones are singing and praising and having a grand old time up there at their real home.

We will always miss our loved ones. A part of us will always long for our loved ones. A part of us will always long to have them by our sides. But we can rest assured that those who die in the Lord are at peace eternally. For me that means so much. Because I love Roderick so very much, I want to see him happy. I want to see him smiling and not crying. I want to see him being loved. I want to see all things good for him to come into full fruition. Now that is exactly what has happened. He is not in a better place like some folks say. He is at home. He is at the best place. The place that each of us should be looking forward to residing. I thank God that Roderick is one of His and because I am too, I will be reunited with him! I miss him so much. And being human, living in this fleshly body, with finite thoughts, I can't help but long for him to be with me rather than with God. But listen to what I am saying. Why would I want him to be with me to satisfy my wants and desires when he is with God - the only one who really matters? I thank God for Roderick, but Roderick belongs to Him not me. The same holds true for your loved one and one day, you too will see and understand what I am talking about - but it's only by traveling the entire journey through grief.

Think about the mansions of the saints of our loved ones. Mansions that were especially prepared for each of them! There is no need to worry or fret because death is no more; crime is no more; hatred is no more; terrorism is no more; evil is no more. Who wouldn't want that for the one we love?

I believe that all the inhabitants of heaven, including our loved ones are preparing for the end of the age here on earth, as we know it. They look forward to our arrival. I believe they join in with God in preparing a place for us as well. But until our time comes, we must travel our journey through grief. We must wait until God takes us home and we will spend eternity with him and our loved ones.

Until that time we must go through some things here on earth. We must experience the good, the bad and the ugly. We must live with the sunshine and the rain of life. We must live with times of hurt and tragedy, disappointment and turmoil. We must live through the storm and the calm. We must live through strife and peace, good and evil. We must live with the bitter and the sweet. We must live with the sting of death until God removes it.

But the good news is that God will return for his own. He will deliver us and bring us through. He alone has decreed and appointed a specific time for all these events spelled out in the book of Revelations and others, to take place. We don't know the date, time or hour, but what we can count on is His Word and His Word tells us that he will come back for us. I just believe my friends, that Heaven is far grander than anything we could ever possibly imagine or dream. So what better place for our loved ones.

Hallelujah, my dear friends! Now isn't this a marvelous, glorious place for our loved ones to reside? Isn't this the place, the perfect place we too shall one day inhabit? Now let us praise God. To God be the glory, great things He has done. Great things He is preparing for those who love Him. Read on into Revelations 22:6a. "The angel said to me, "These words can be trusted and are true. Verse 7: "Listen! I am coming soon! Happy is the one who obeys the words of prophecy in this book." (Bible passages from the New Century Version).

I don't know about you, but I stand in awe and wonderment over having this revelation knowledge. I am, therefore, thankful to God almighty for His love, His mercy, and His grace and for shedding His precious blood so that we, our loved ones, all believers in Christ will have such a magnificent home on high forever more!

Don't you remember that conversation Martha had with Jesus when she was going through her journey of grief after her brother, Lazarus died? "Lord, she said, "if you had been here, my brother would not have died."

Jesus said, "Your brother will rise and live again."

Martha answered, "I know that he will rise and live again in the resurrection on the last day."

Jesus said to her, "I am the resurrection and the life. Those who believe in me will have life even if they die, and everyone who believes in me will never die..." (John 11:21-25 New Century Version)

Won't you stop reading for a moment and give Him some praise even in the midst of your pain!

Life for me has changed forever
My love has left me all alone
Now what shall I do
with all that we shared
Because all of what we had
is now gone.

I will go on living
Try to make a difference
in this world
I'll even share
the precious Love of God
To some lost man, woman,
Boy and girl.

Shelia E. Lipsey

14

DEATH CHANGES LIFE

On our journey through grief our lives will change in some shape or form. Since Roderick's death, I do not view life as I once did. Now I try, with God's unfailing help, to live each day for all that it is worth. I ask Him to order my steps, to direct my path, to lead me through this valley that overshadows me. I have become more keenly aware of His presence and His glory and majesty. I am now able to give Him more of the praise He truly deserves. I am more at peace as I ponder on His marvelous works. Because I have placed my trust in Him, I know that He is guiding my every step, even the steps of pain that I walk through, even this journey through grief.

I did not say that I don't experience the pain, the loss and the hurt from losing Roderick. I said that I am now beginning to view life and living in a different way. I am now beginning to see God for who He really is. I am now beginning to feel His presence fill up my loneliness with His unconditional love.

You too, can allow Him to change you, to change your thinking, to change your walking, to change your talking. Live for Him so that you may die In Him. Hold on to His unwavering hand and become mighty in spirit, victorious over your trials, living a life that is centered on Him.

It is a fact, my dear friends, that we too, will make that same journey as our loved ones already have. Death is inevitable. Whether death comes as a result of sickness, murder, old age, birth defects or accident, or a terrorist attack, death is coming for each of us. I don't know about you, but I want to be found going about the work of the Lord. I don't want to be found still harboring anger and bitterness. I don't want to be found still holding on to unforgiveness and hate. I don't want to be found still cutting myself off from God. Instead, I want to be found living the life He has prepared for me while I am here on this earth. I want to be found holy, righteous and full of the spirit of God. I want to be found going about doing His work. I want to be found praying and lifting people up. I want to be found rejoicing in the God of my salvation and in the God Roderick had come to love so much. Don't you?

On your journey though grief, my friends there will still be times when you may feel as if you are on a roller-coaster ride. There are days when you will be up and days when you will be down. There will be times when your tears will flow and your heart will ache. There will be times when you will cry over the loss of your loved one and there will be times when you will be able to smile when you think on the precious memories he/she left behind for you. There will be times when you will feel burdened and times when you will stand tall in your trust and faith in God.

It has been as I said, over five years since Roderick's death. I still find myself sinking, especially during special days or special moments that I would like to have him here with me to share. There are other times when I can talk or think about him and a tender and loving smile envelops my face. There are times I am so very lonely living without him and there are times when I rejoice because he is with our Heavenly Father, the Master of us all. But now, during these moments along my journey through grief, I know that I am not alone. God is yet with me; and my dear friends He is with you too.

"Although the fig tree shall not blossom, neither shall fruit be in the vines; the labour of the olive shall fail, and the fields shall yield no meat, the flock shall be cut off from the fold and there shall be no herd in the stalls; Yet I will rejoice in the Lord, I will joy in the God of my salvation. The Lord God is my strength and he will make my feet like hinds feet; and he will make me to walk upon mine high places." (Habakkuk 3:17-19 KJV)

He desires to do for you what he did for Habakkuk and what He is doing for me. Won't you let Him?

What we once enjoyed
And deeply loved
We can never lose.
For all that
We love deeply
Becomes part of us.

Helen Keller

15

WHAT ABOUT THESE FEELINGS

Someone you loved has died now. Someone who was a very important part of your life, your well-being, your world. Someone who gave you a sense of joy, laughter, and love. Someone that meant the entire world to you. There are so many feelings going on inside of you. There are so many feelings going on inside of me too, my friend. That someone is no longer with you here in the physical. You'll never hear their laughter. You'll never hear their words or funny jokes or see their silly smile. You'll never again wipe away their tears when they were in pain or share in their times of sadness. That person, your loved one, has been removed from your presence now.

What do you do? You ask me if life goes on even after losing someone you love? Yes, life does go on. But life will never be the same again. That is what hurts. That is what pains you. No matter what you are feeling, your feelings are yours, and yours alone. They are not wrong feelings or bad feelings. They are your feelings. Don't even begin to try to put a time frame on how you feel. Don't allow anyone else to put a time frame on your feelings either. Just feel. This is how you prepare yourself to live life without your loved one. This is how you cope and deal with all that has happened and is happening. Allow yourself to feel.

I have found out a remarkable thing since I have allowed myself to feel. That is, that love does transcend. Love never ends. I feel that now. I know that the love Roderick and I shared will go on forever, for always. I feel him in my spirit. I feel his love breathing on me, filling me, smiling on me. Death cannot bring what we had to an end. Death has no power over love, especially a love allowed and sent by God. Death is merely a physical separation but it can never break us, our spirits, our hearts or our love apart.

Since I have begun to allow my feelings to surface, I now can feel Roderick with me, close to me, still loving me. I can still feel my heart race wildly at the thought of him. I can still feel his smile and see his love. Some folks don't understand this and perhaps never will. But even that's okay. My feelings are mine and mine alone.

Your feelings are yours and yours alone. Death cannot rob you of what is in your heart. Death can never take away the love that you have for your loved one. Death cannot destroy the love your loved one has for you. I know it hurts. I know it's hard. I know sorrow seems to enshroud you and swallow you. But, I am here to tell you, my friend that we will make it. Our lives will go on—even after losing someone we love; but only if we travel our journey of grief with God.

16

THE JUNIPER TREE EFFECT

We've all been there at one time or another. Depression, crises, broken relationships, lost jobs, illness on and on the cycle goes. The Juniper Tree has many visitors and is called by many names – but still when it is all over, I call it The Juniper Tree Effect.

When you lose a loved one in death, I can guarantee you that you, like me, will have your share of the Juniper Tree experience. Let me shed a little light on where I got the name.

In the Old Testament bible, Elijah was a strong man of God. He had great faith. He had that kind of mountain moving faith. Yet when Jezebel said she would get him and kill him, he quickly fled. He kept on running hard and fast, trying to escape her clutches. After much running and once he thought he was far enough away from her evil reach, he rested under a juniper tree. He sat under that juniper tree and there he stayed. He slept under that juniper tree. He hid out under that juniper tree. Safe from Jezebel, the evil one. Here is the story as told in 1 Kings 19:1-3. "Now Ahab told Jezebel everything Elijah had done and how he had killed all the prophets with the sword. So Jezebel sent a messenger to Elijah to say, "May the gods deal with me, be it ever so severely, if by this time tomorrow I do not make your life like that of one of them. Elijah was afraid and ran for his life." Elijah ran until he reached the desert. He spotted a Juniper tree and fell down under it, pleading with God that he might die. He told the Lord, "I have had enough Lord, take my life... "(Vs. 4).

Losing a loved one can put even the strongest of us Christians under the juniper tree. We can find ourselves experiencing what I call the Juniper Tree Effect. Staying in the house away from family and friends becomes our juniper tree. Shying away from new relationships becomes our juniper tree. Keeping everyone at arms length, so no one can pierce our hearts ever again becomes our juniper tree. Holding our hurt and heartache inside ourselves can become our juniper tree.

The Juniper Tree Effect is a phase that can be a normal experience, a normal part of our journey through grief, as long as we do not become too content under the shelter of the juniper tree.

God wants to deliver us from underneath the juniper tree of grief, sadness and spiritual depression. He stands ready to send help to us and for us. Just as he sent the angel to Elijah, he will send his angels to deliver us.

When we are on our journey through grief, there might be moments when we feel just as Elijah felt. We are tired and sad and broken and hurting. We just don't see how we can take anymore. You see, instead of allowing Elijah to fall into death, the Lord sent an angel to touch him and awake him. The angel told him to "get up and eat." God provided food and water for Elijah. Though Elijah found himself eating and drinking the food and water the angel of the Lord brought, he still sunk back down into his depression, again falling asleep under the Juniper Tree.

That is exactly how you might find yourself. One moment you might feel the presence of the Lord. You might even experience a little strength, but soon you're back underneath the juniper tree of grief and its branches hold you even tighter in its grip, clinging to your heart.

The angel of the Lord came back a second time and touched Elijah. Again the angel provided Elijah with food and drink. This time Elijah got up and his strength began to be renewed so much so that he was able to move from under the juniper tree and travel for forty days and forty nights…(vs8-9)

You too will find that you will be able to, in your own time, move forward or move away from underneath your juniper tree. Elijah still had his up and down periods and so will you and so do I. I have come to believe that I will always ride a roller coaster. There are those times I am hit with a fresh new onslaught of grief when I think of my beloved Roderick. There are other times, I will travel the journey and be strengthened.

You too, can make it my friend. But only the Lord is able to give you that strength. Only He is able to move you from underneath the Juniper Tree Effect. Won't you call on Him, the only one who can deliver you and the only one who is continually delivering me! Praise God from whom all blessings flow!

17

DOES LIFE REALLY GO ON— *EVEN AFTER LOSING SOMEONE YOU LOVE?*

After Roderick's death, I heard this from well-meaning people over and over again. Shelia, remember, "Life goes on." Each time I heard it, I became angrier and angrier. How dare anyone tell me that life goes on after losing the man I loved. How dare them believe that my life will continue as if Roderick didn't exist. I did not understand how or why anyone could possibly think that this would make me feel better. It did just the opposite. I thought to myself, "Yeah, right, sure." They weren't fooling me. After all, most of the people who told me "life goes on" still had their mates, or loved ones with them. They had no knowledge of what I was experiencing over Roderick's death. I would look around me and see couples happily strolling hand in hand, smiling at each other, hugging each other, and loving each other. Of course, it was easy for any one of them to tell me, "Life goes on." Sure, it was easy for a mother to tell Roderick's mother that everything would be alright when that woman still had her only son living and breathing and walking this earth while Norma had lost hers. Sure it's easy for others to say that things will work out just fine when their brother or sister or mate or child is still with them everyday. Oh how I despised these people so. I became quite offended and defensive. I didn't want to ever hear that phrase ever again – *life goes on*. I have only recently begun to be able to hear these words without so much anger and resentment welling up inside of me.

I am now coming to the realization that my "life does go on" but it is a changed life. It is a totally new and different life I live now without Roderick. Quite soon after Roderick's death I enrolled in college to study for my degree in Business only to consume some of the empty, lonely hours. But no matter what the reason I chose to attend college, I realize that my life is going on. When I saturated myself in study and graduated magna cum laude I realized that my life is going on.

I have even become more aware of the presence of God, paying less attention to worldly pleasures and events. My life goes on and that means it includes me thinking of Roderick each day in some way. I remember the strength he gave me. I remember the love he shared so openly and unconditionally with me. I remember his powerful, spirit-filled prayers to God. I remember his words of encouragement to me. I even go on because I know that he wants me to go on living.

You too, may not believe at this point that life goes on after losing someone you love. But it does my friend. That life might be complete with pain and sorrow and the thoughts of your loved one might consume your mind. But life goes on. It seems like an old tired cliché. But no matter how we try to avoid it, it is a true statement.

Now we can determine how our life will go on without our loved one. Will we live lives consumed with the fire of bitterness and anger and unforgiveness? Or will we live our lives carrying the memories of our loved ones forever in our hearts? Will we go out and do positive things that will help us on our journey through grief? Or will we decide to wallow in our sorrow forever?

As for me, I am trying to let go and let God. I am trying to live each day in a way that is pleasing to God. I want to be bold in proclaiming that even in the middle of this madness that God is the head of my life.

This is a process my friends. It does not happen for most of us overnight. There is not a set time frame. Allow yourself to take it one day at a time. Think of some of the things that were important to your loved one and perhaps try to bring those things into full fruition where they can glorify God. At the same time, it can bring a sense of purpose and a sense of healing into your lives.

I began working in my church with the very outreach ministry Roderick was involved in. Roderick loved reaching out to people, helping people and just loving people. I decided to become involved in the outreach ministry as a way of carrying on a great work that he enjoyed. It brought joy into my life. I felt close to Roderick. I felt that I was doing something he would be proud of me for doing. I felt his spirit leading me and pushing me to keep going.

God wants us to live victorious lives. And we can. We too can come to know that it is true, "life goes on." How are we going to live it is the question? Won't you take one step at a time, one moment at a time and once again begin to live – live for God? Live with the knowledge of his resurrection power and you too will make it on your journey through grief.

"But we do not want you to be uninformed, brethren, about those who are asleep, so that you will not grieve as do the rest who have no hope.

For if we believe that Jesus died and rose again, even so God will bring with Him those who have fallen asleep in Jesus.

For this we say to you by the word of the Lord, that we, who are alive and remain until the coming of the Lord, will not precede those who have fallen asleep.

For the Lord Himself will descend from heaven with a shout, with the voice of the archangel and with the trumpet of God, and the dead in Christ will rise first. Then we who are alive and remain will be caught up together with them in the clouds to meet the Lord in the air, and so we shall always be with the Lord. Therefore comfort one another with these words. 1 Thessalonians 4:13-18 NIV."

My friends, the journey will not be an easy one. You will make good friends with pain along the way. You will come to know heartache and heartbreak very well. You will start to find yourself becoming closer to the tears that seem to constantly stream down your face. That is part of this journey of grief. But as believers; as children of the most high God, you will also encounter strength along the journey. You'll find solace along the journey. You'll find acceptance and forgiveness along the journey. You'll find that God does love you and that He loves your loved one even more than you or I can ever begin to conceive or understand. You'll begin to realize that God is yet with you. He is the one who is undergirding you. He alone is the one that is keeping you up; holding you up. He alone is the one that is picking you up, storing your tears; and bathing your aching heart with his love. You are not alone. He is with YOU. He is with me. And your loved one is with him. The journey, the journey through grief is one that you will never travel alone for God is by your side. Cry out to him; reach up to him; cling to him; call out to him; hold on to him; latch on to him; talk to him. He is able. He is by your side every step of the way. One day you'll awaken; one day you'll open your eyes and you will know just like I now know - that because of our faith and our belief - life does go on even after losing someone you love.

SPIRIT BOOSTER PRAYER

In the midst of fear and trembling, in the midst of this journey through grief, the Holy Spirit reminds me that you God, are my father, and are yet with me. I may not feel your presence right now Father because the grip of pain and grief is holding me tight within its powerful clutches. Yet, I know you are surrounding me in Your love. You have told me that you will never leave me or forsake me. My inner spirit tells me that you are keeping me through this difficult time.

I know within that everything You allow to come into my life, to pass through my life, to overshadow my life; even though it appears to be defeating me, that you dear Father, will work it out for my good because You know I do love You; but more importantly because You love me just like you love my loved one who has gone to live with you in that beautiful place you have prepared for those who love You. But Father, even though I know this, I am still frightened. I am still in tremendous pain over the death of my loved one LORD. I hear bitterness and anger, despair and doubt pounding at my heart's door.

I thank you, Dear Lord because you don't hold these thoughts and feelings against me. You understand me; know all about me, you know the pain and sorrow that envelops me now. You love me with an unconditional, unfathomable love.

Father, I don't see how I will make it through this painful moment in my life, but I know you already have it all worked out because your plans for me are plans for my good, plans of prosperity, hope and love.

Oh, Lord, the storm is yet raging. I see no end to the night. Remind me over and over again that You are the master of even the darkest storms of life. You are my Prince of Peace, My Wonderful Counselor. You are My rock, My fortress, and My mighty shield. Guide me oh thy great Jehovah. Amen.

THE WORD OF GOD –
FOR THE PEOPLE OF GOD

Locate the scriptures below in your bible. Read, ponder and pray on these passages of scriptures. As you do, write down your thoughts and your feelings about each one. Don't hold back anything, whether negative or positive. I have found that they have actually provided me with healing, comfort, reassurance and encouragement during my journey through grief. It is my earnest, heart-filled hope and prayer that they will do the same for you, my friends.

1. **Psalm 116:15** – Precious in the sight of the Lord is the death of his saints.

2. **Philippians 2:23** – I am torn between the two; I desire to depart and be with Christ, which is better.

3. **1 Thessalonians: 4:13** – Brothers, we do not want you to be ignorant about those who "fall asleep," or to grieve like the rest of men, who have no hope.

4. **Job 14:5** – Man's days are determined; you have decreed the number of his months and have set limits he cannot exceed.

5. **Psalm 34:4** – The Lord is close to the brokenhearted and saves those who are crushed in spirit.

6. **Psalm 147:3** He heals the brokenhearted and binds up their wounds.

7. **Lamentations 4:18** – ...Our end was near, our days were numbered for our end had come.

8. **Matt 5:4** – Blessed are those who mourn, for they will be comforted.

9. **Matt 10:28** – Do not be afraid of those who kill the body but cannot kill the soul, Rather, be afraid of the One who can destroy both soul and body in hell.

10. **Luke 16:22** – The time came when the beggar died and the angels carried him to Abraham's side.

11. **l Corinthians 2:9** – No eye has seen, no ear has heard, no mind has conceived what God has prepared for those who love him.

12. **l Corinthians 15:45** – If there is a natural body, there is also a spiritual body.

13. **2 Corinthians 5:1** – Now we know that if the earthly tent we live in is destroyed, we have a building from God, an eternal house in heaven, not built by human hands.

14. **2 Corinthians 5:6** – Therefore we are always confident and know that as long as we are at home in the body we are away from the Lord.

15. **Philippians 2:21** – For me to live is Christ, and to die is gain.

My friends, if you by chance are reading this book, and you do not have a personal relationship with God, then I extend this invitation of acceptance to you. If you have not yet trusted God as your Lord and Savior, as the giver of eternal life, you can do so right now. We do not know the second, the minute, the hour, the moment or day that God will come to claim us. Will you be ready?

God says,
"If you confess with your mouth, Jesus is Lord, and believe in your heart that God raised Jesus from the dead, you will be saved. For it is with your heart that you believe and are justified, and it is with your mouth that you confess and are SAVED." (Romans 10:9-10 NIV)

WORKS CITED

Lewis, C. S. *A Grief Observed*. New York: Bantam, 1961.

Other Books by Shelia E. Lipsey

Inspirational Novels
Always, Now and Forever
Into Each Life...release date Winter 2003

www.spiritbooster.com